HOW TO DRAW
WARRIORS

Steve Beaumont

PowerKiDS
press
New York

Published in 2008 by The Rosen Publishing Group, Inc.
29 East 21st Street, New York, NY 10010

Copyright © 2008 Arcturus Publishing Ltd

Artwork and text: Steve Beaumont
Editor (Arcturus): Alex Woolf
Editor (Rosen): Jennifer Way
Designer: Jane Hawkins

Library of Congress Cataloging-in-Publication Data

Beaumont, Steve.
  How to draw warriors / Steve Beaumont.
     p. cm. — (Drawing fantasy art)
  Includes index.
  ISBN-13: 978-1-4042-3858-9 (library binding)
  ISBN-10: 1-4042-3858-1 (libray binding)
  1. Heroes in art—Juvenile literature. 2. Fantasy in art—Juvenile literature. 3. Drawing—
Technique—Juvenile literature. I. Title.
  NC825.H45B43 2008
  743.4—dc22
                              2007001620

Printed in U.S.A. by Bang Printing, Minnesota

Contents

Introduction

If you have picked up this book, you are probably a big fan of sword-and-sorcery movies, books, or games. You may be one of those fans who enjoys the genre so much that you would like to try creating some magical characters for yourself. If so, this book will help you get started on the right path.

One of the best things about drawing warriors and other fantasy figures is that, apart from the basic rules of anatomy and perspective, there are not many rules. In fantasy art, no one can tell you that a character's sword is the wrong shape or his hair is the wrong color. These are products of your imagination and you can draw them exactly as you please!

Warriors

Warriors play a central role in many myths and legends. They are usually brave and heroic characters who go on dangerous adventures to right wrongs, fight dragons, and rescue people. The most interesting warriors often have some flaw in their character. Sir Lancelot's weakness was his love for the wife of his king. Samson was undone by his own pride.

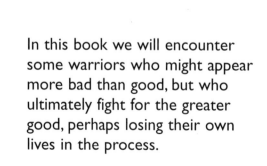

In this book we will encounter some warriors who might appear more bad than good, but who ultimately fight for the greater good, perhaps losing their own lives in the process.

Equipment

To start, you will need the tools of the trade. You must have decent materials and equipment to produce high-quality illustrations.

Paper

For your practice sketches, buy some cheap paper from a stationery shop. When practicing ink drawing, use line art paper, which can be purchased from an art or craft shop.

For painting with watercolors, use watercolor paper. Most art shops stock a large range of weights and sizes.

Pencils

Get a good range of lead pencils ranging from soft to hard. Hard-lead pencils last longer and leave fewer smudges on your paper. Soft-lead ones leave darker marks on the paper and wear down more quickly. Number 4 pencils are good medium-range pencils for beginners.

For fine, detailed work, mechanical pencils are ideal. These are available in a range of lead thicknesses, 0.5 mm being a good middle range.

Pens

For inking, use either a ballpoint or a simple dip pen and nib. For coloring, experiment with the wide variety of felt-tips on the market.

Markers

These are very versatile pens that, with practice, can give very pleasing results.

Brushes

Some artists like to use a fine brush for inking line work. This takes a bit more practice to master, but the results can be very satisfying. If you want to try your hand at brushwork, you will need some good-quality sable brushes.

Watercolors and gouache

Most art shops will also stock a wide range of these products, from student to professional quality.

Inks

Any good brand will do.

Eraser

There are three types of eraser: rubber, plastic, and putty. Try all three to see which you prefer.

You may also want to find something to sharpen your pencils!

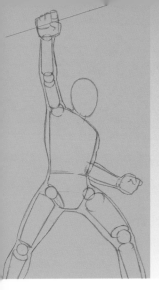

Basic Construction

Here is a pencil drawing of a brave warrior striking a heroic pose. How do we get from a blank piece of paper to this? The answer lies in mastering the basic stick figure. If you can draw the stick figure effectively, everything else flows from there. This skill is also important when drawing action scenes, in which your work needs to be full of energy.

The sketches below show the stages of the process that resulted in the drawing on the previous page.

Step 1
First, do a few loose sketches, called thumbnails, to establish the basic shape of the figure. Then make a larger drawing of your chosen sketch.

Step 2
The basic construction of the human form can be broken down into geometric shapes, such as squares circles, and triangles. When drawing these shapes, it helps to think of them as solid objects, such as spheres, egg shapes, cubes, and cylinders. Now try using these shapes to flesh out your stick figure.

Step 3
Finally, add a smoother finish to the stick figure.

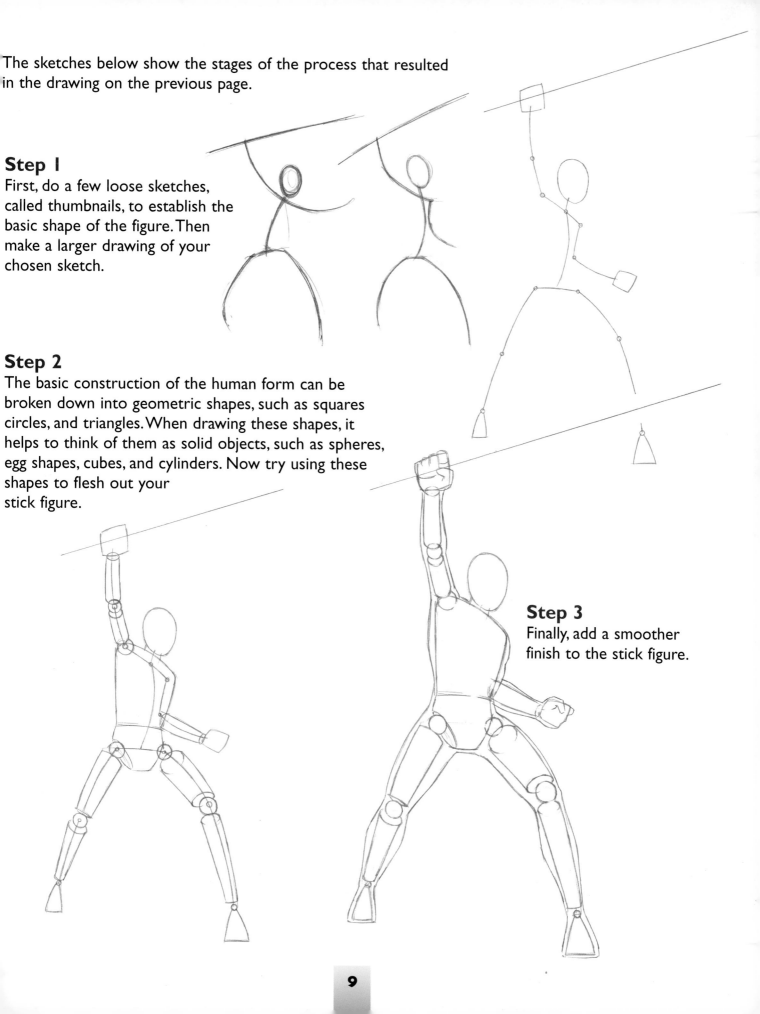

Faces, Hands, and Feet

As with all character drawing, so much of the personality of a warrior is in the face. It is therefore worth spending a bit of time working on your techniques in this important area. Hands and feet are also important in action illustrations and can be tricky to get right.

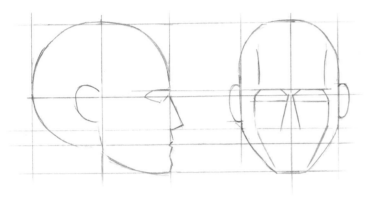

Constructing the face

The human head generally fits into a square. Note that the nose and chin stick out slightly. It may help to divide the square into quarters. The eyes generally sit halfway above the center line, with the nose taking up half the depth of the bottom square. Notice how the ears line up in relation to the eyes and nose.

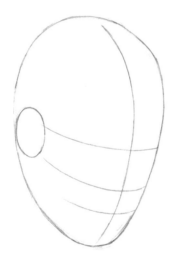

Male face

Our hero is looking down and to the side, so draw an upside-down egg shape for his head, and place it at a slight angle. Draw in lines to help you position the eyes, nose, and mouth. It helps to think of it as an egg while you do this.

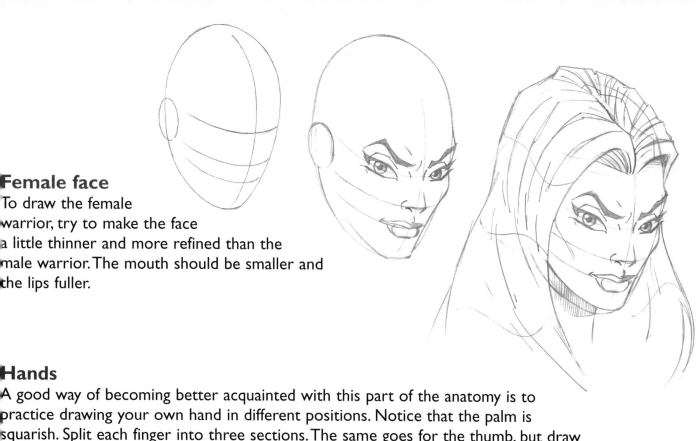

Female face

To draw the female
warrior, try to make the face
a little thinner and more refined than the
male warrior. The mouth should be smaller and
the lips fuller.

Hands

A good way of becoming better acquainted with this part of the anatomy is to
practice drawing your own hand in different positions. Notice that the palm is
squarish. Split each finger into three sections. The same goes for the thumb, but draw
its base section as a large triangle. This is not anatomically correct, but it does help
when sketching hand movements.

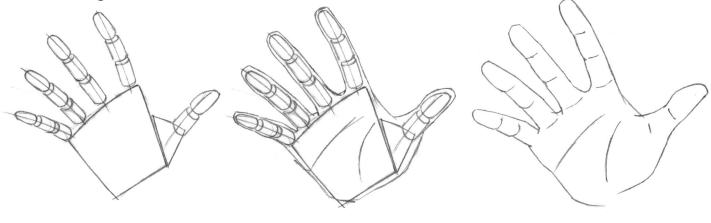

Feet

This is a part of the body
with which a lot of young
artists struggle. In most
cases, just think of the foot
as a sort of triangular
shape. Use these examples
as a guide to its
construction.

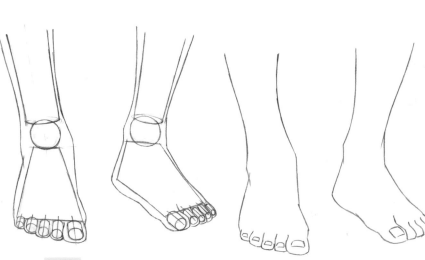

Male Warrior

Although he is a hero, this particular warrior is also bordering on the barbaric. He is a true fighter who lives for the thrill of battle. Muscular and brutish, he will stop at nothing to defeat his enemies.

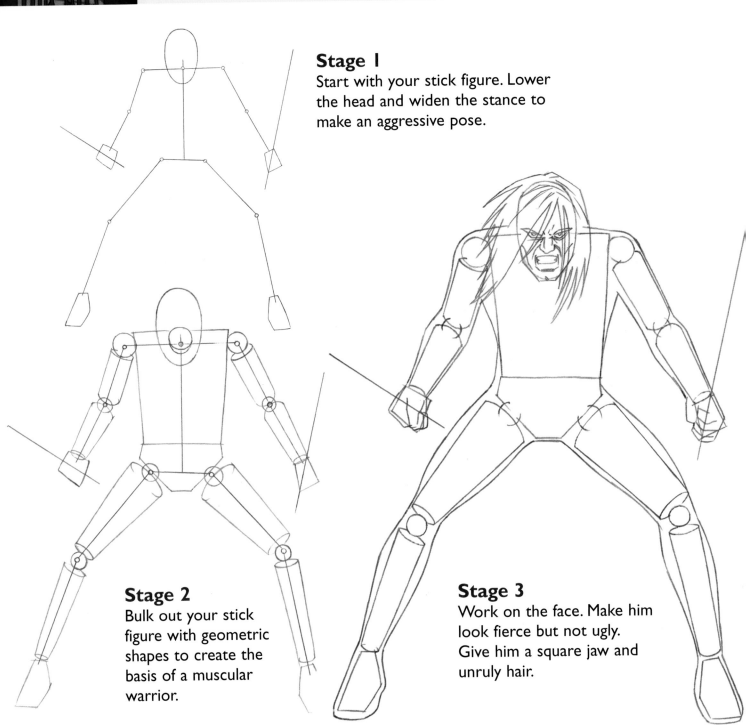

Stage 1
Start with your stick figure. Lower the head and widen the stance to make an aggressive pose.

Stage 2
Bulk out your stick figure with geometric shapes to create the basis of a muscular warrior.

Stage 3
Work on the face. Make him look fierce but not ugly. Give him a square jaw and unruly hair.

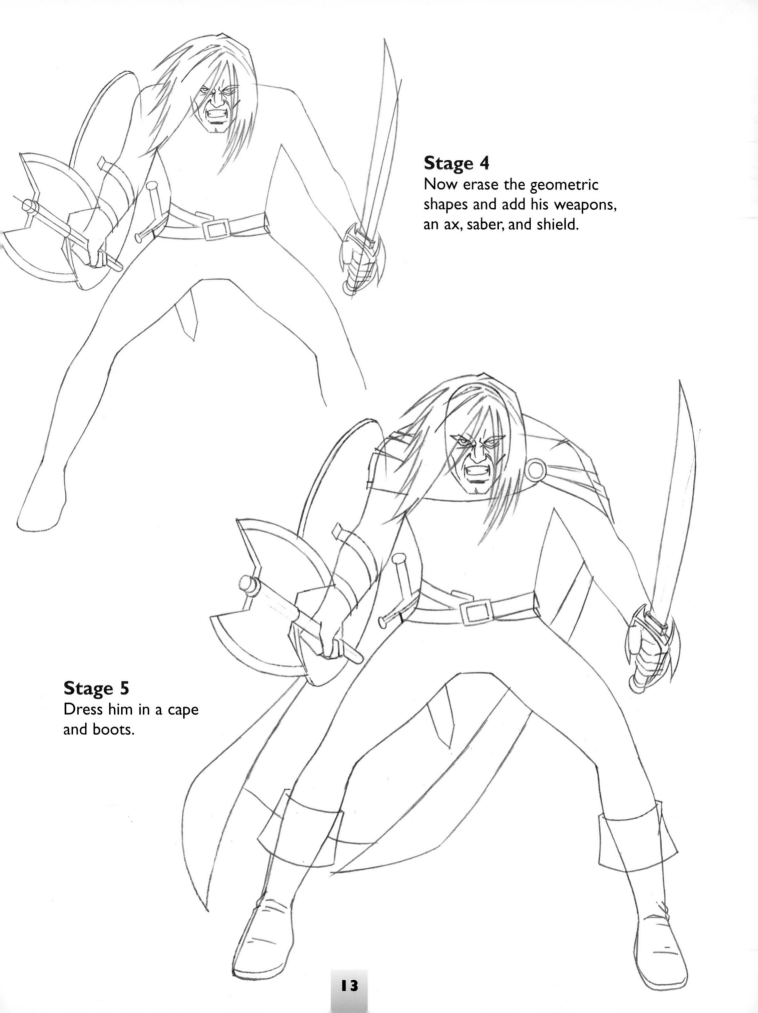

Stage 4
Now erase the geometric
shapes and add his weapons,
an ax, saber, and shield.

Stage 5
Dress him in a cape
and boots.

13

Stage 6
Add a leather breastplate with a crest on it. Design your own if you wish.

Stage 7
Clean up the earlier pencil work and add in some shading to give your figure solidity.

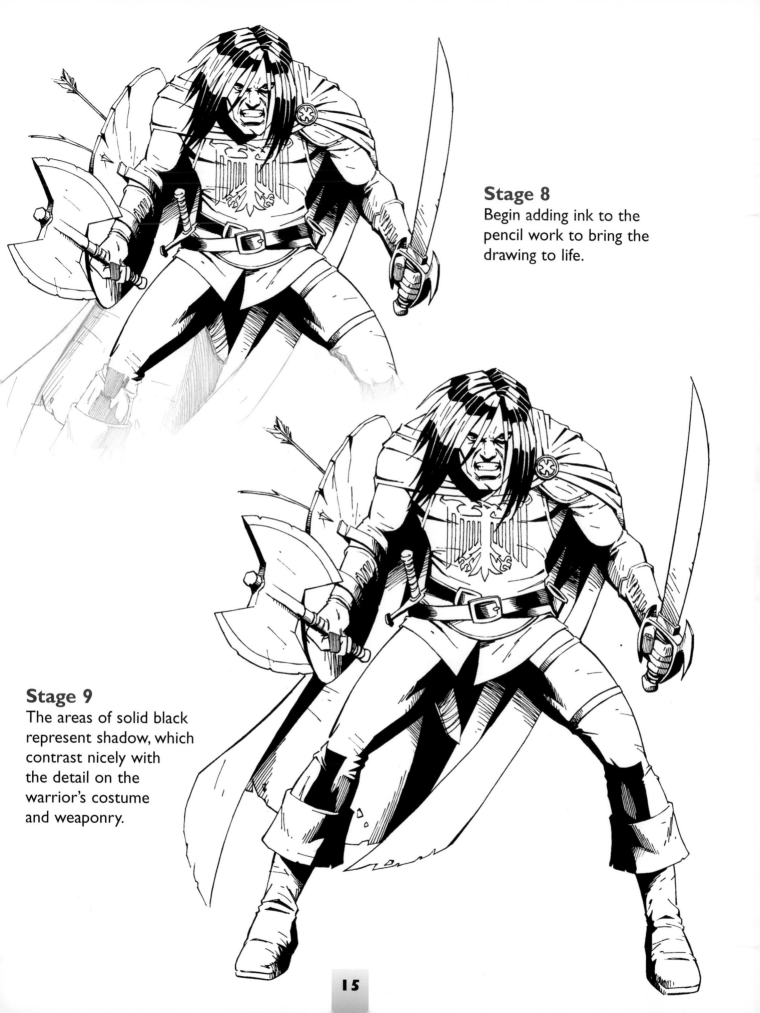

Stage 8
Begin adding ink to the pencil work to bring the drawing to life.

Stage 9
The areas of solid black represent shadow, which contrast nicely with the detail on the warrior's costume and weaponry.

Stage 10

You can color your drawing if you like, using markers, felt-tips, or watercolors. Lay down each color in one continuous wash if you can, applying the color as smoothly as possible.

Keeping to dull, darker colors will add to the overall impression of a savage warrior about to attack. You would not want to be on the other end of that sword, would you?

Female Warrior

Who says guys have all the orc-slaying fun? Women can swing an ax just as well. History is littered with female warriors, from Boudicca, Queen of the Britons, to Joan of Arc, the fearless leader of the French.

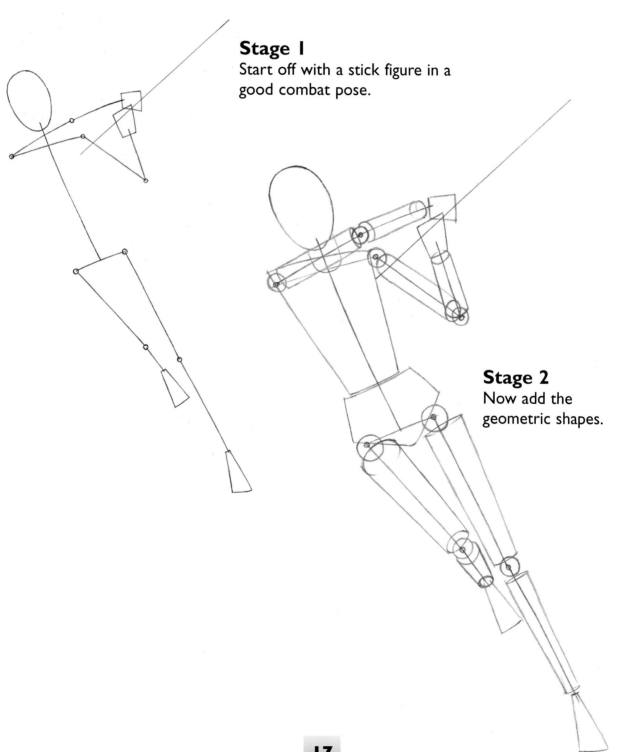

Stage 1
Start off with a stick figure in a good combat pose.

Stage 2
Now add the geometric shapes.

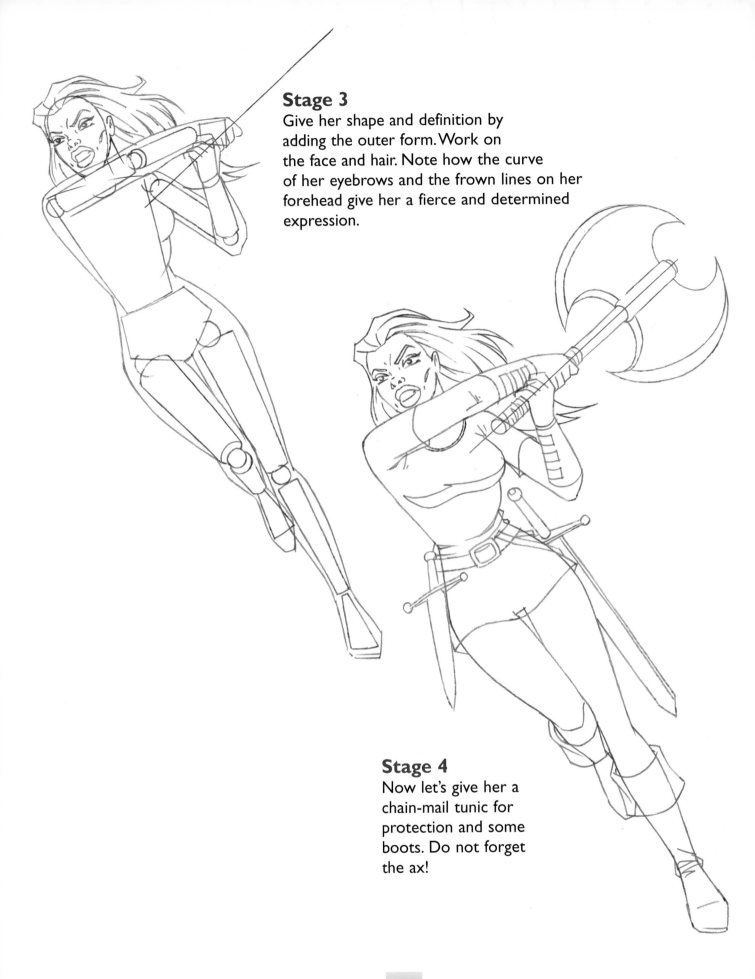

Stage 3

Give her shape and definition by adding the outer form. Work on the face and hair. Note how the curve of her eyebrows and the frown lines on her forehead give her a fierce and determined expression.

Stage 4

Now let's give her a chain-mail tunic for protection and some boots. Do not forget the ax!

Stage 5
Here is the finished pencil drawing. Note the added detail on her chain mail, weaponry, boots, and hair.

Stage 6
Now clean up the line work and carefully ink over the pencil drawing, making sure you keep the lines crisp and clean.

Stage 7
Note that there are very few solid areas. Although the final ink drawing is strong and dynamic, some delicate line work helps maintain a feminine look.

Stage 8

Now you can color your drawing.
The flame-red hair emphasizes our heroine's
warrior nature. Traditionally, female warriors are
illustrated using lighter colors, with fewer dark
or dull tones.

Warrior on Horseback

This hero appears more savage than noble. He is a nomadic warrior on horseback, who roams the land in search of adventure.

Stage 1

This image may look hard to draw, but it is easier when broken down into stages. Because the skeleton of a horse is not as simple as the human skeleton, the horse will be broken down into a frame that is not technically correct. This will make drawing it much easier. Start with your stick figure.

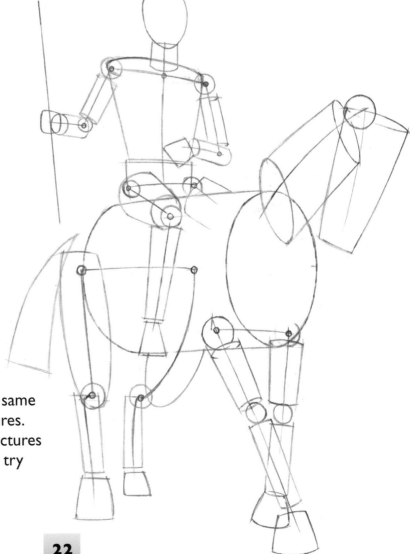

Stage 2

Note how a horse can be formed from the same geometric shapes as a human figure. A long, bulky cylinder is used for the horse's body, while the legs follow the same ball-joint construction used for human figures. When drawing animals, it helps to study pictures of the creature that you wish to draw and try breaking it down into geometric shapes.

Stage 3

Draw a smoother outer form over the geometric shapes. Narrow eyes and a square jaw create the right mood for this warrior.

Stage 4

Now erase the geometric shapes and add a full head of unruly black hair plus a fur around his shoulders and a leather vest. Also add the horse's mane.

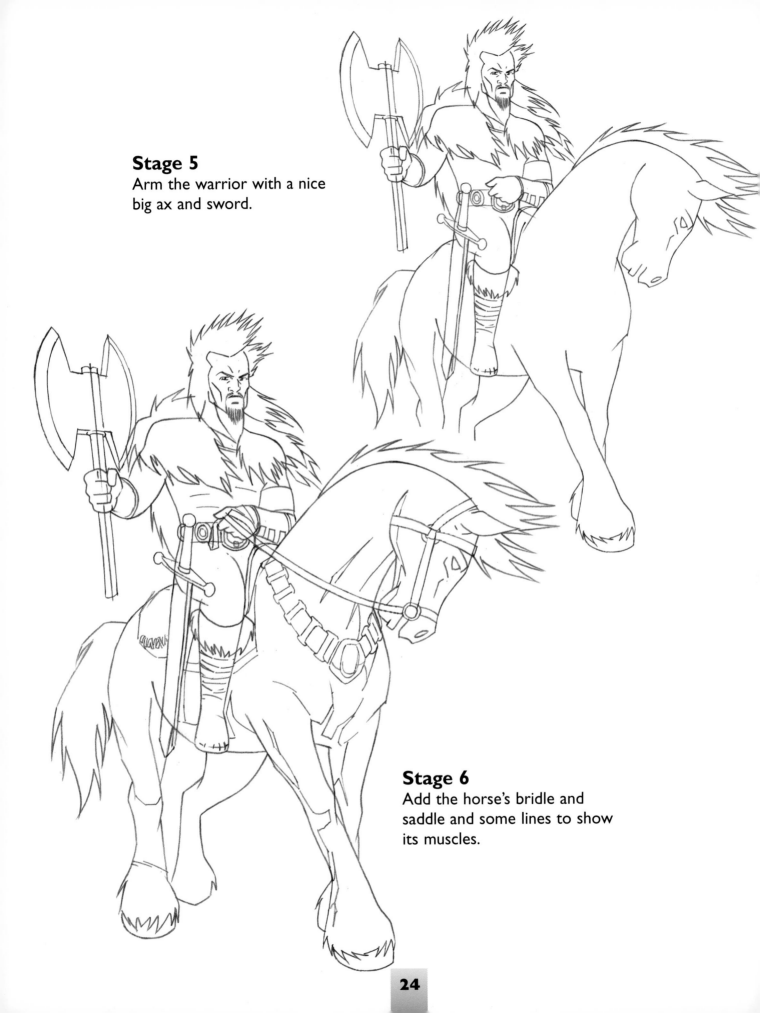

Stage 5
Arm the warrior with a nice big ax and sword.

Stage 6
Add the horse's bridle and saddle and some lines to show its muscles.

Stage 7

Put in the final details to your pencil drawing. Shade the darker areas and clean up any rough line work.

Stage 8

Now start the inking. Be careful not to lose any of the smaller details by overdoing it.

25

Stage 9

Note the use of solid black on areas such as the horse's rear legs to create depth. The deep shadows add to the sense of danger in both warrior and horse.

Stage 10

Although it may be tempting to use only dark colors with this warrior, try mixing up the darker tones with pale browns and yellows. This will keep the image from looking flat. A light blue wash has been added to the ax, making it appear stronger and heavier.

Warrior Gallery

Here are some examples of warriors of all types, doing what they do best, preparing for battle. Try drawing some of them yourself by breaking them down into stages, as we have done on the previous pages. You can also use them as inspiration for creating your own characters.

Glossary

anatomy (uh-NA-tuh-mee) The physical structure of a human or other organism.

ball joint (BOL JOYNT) Also known as a ball-and-socket joint, this is a joint in which the rounded end of one part fits into a cup-shaped socket on the other.

barbaric (bahr-BER-ik) Uncivilized and primitive.

Boudicca (BOO-dih-kuh) A queen of the Britons and ruler of the Iceni tribe, who led her forces in a revolt against the Romans in 60–61 CE.

bridle (BRY-dul) A set of leather straps fitted to a horse's head, including the bit and the reins.

brutish (BROO-tish) Like an animal.

chain mail (CHAYN MAYL) Interlinked rings of metal forming a flexible piece of armor.

cylinder (SIH-len-der) A shape with straight sides and circular ends of equal size.

dynamic (dy-NA-mik) Full of energy.

geometric shape (jee-uh-MEH-trik SHAYP) A simple shape, such as a cube, sphere, or cylinder.

gouache (GWAHSH) A mixture of nontransparent watercolor paint and gum.

Joan of Arc (JOHN UV AHRK) A French national heroine who led the French armies against the English during the Hundred Years War, relieving the besieged city of Orléans in 1429.

mechanical pencil (mih-KA-nih-kul PENT-sul) A pencil with replaceable lead that may be advanced as needed.

nomadic (noh-MA-dik) Describing a person who wanders from one place to another.

orc (ORK) A member of an imaginary race of ugly, warlike, and evil creatures.

perspective (per-SPEK-tiv) In drawing, changing the relative size and appearance of objects to allow for the effects of distance.

saber (SAY-ber) A heavy sword with a slightly curved blade that is sharp on one edge.

Samson (SAM-sun) An Israelite warrior from Biblical times, famous for his great strength.

Sir Lancelot (SUR LANT-suh-lot) A legendary warrior, the most famous of King Arthur's knights.

sphere (SFEER) An object shaped like a ball.

stance (STANTS) The way a person stands.

stick figure (STIK FIH-gyur) A simple drawing of a person with single lines for the torso, arms, and legs.

watercolor (WO-ter-kuh-ler) Paint made by mixing pigments, substances that give something its color, with water.

Further Reading

Books

Drawing and Painting Fantasy Figures: From the Imagination to the Page by Finlay Cowan (David and Charles, 2004)

Draw Medieval Fantasies by Damon J. Reinagle (Peel Productions, 1995)

How to Draw Comic Book Bad Guys and Gals by Christopher Hart (Watson-Guptill Publications, 1998)

How to Draw Comic Book Heroes and Villains by Christopher Hart (Watson-Guptill Publications, 2001)

How to Draw Fantasy Characters by Christopher Hart (Watson-Guptill Publications, 1999)

How to Draw Manga Heroes and Villains by Peter Gray (The Rosen Publishing Group, 2006)

Web Sites

Due to the changing nature of Internet links, PowerKids Press has developed an online list of Web sites related to the subject of this book. This site is updated regularly. Please use this link to access the list: www.powerkidslinks.com/dfa/warr/

Index